A Child's Book of Animal Poems and Blessings

Collected by Eliza Blanchard

Illustrated by Joyce Hesselberth

Praise God for the animals
for the colors of them,
for the spots and stripes of them,
for the patches and plains of them,
their claws and paws.

—*Lynn Warren*

I throw myself to the left
I turn myself to the right.
I am the fish
Who glides in the water, who glides,
Who twists himself, who leaps.
Everything lives, everything dances,
everything sings.

—*African pygmy*

For dragonflies, butterflies,
Caterpillars on leaves,
Lizards, wild turkeys, and tigers and deer,
We give thanks!

For sunset and seashells
And starfish and sand,
Octopus, jellyfish, and hammerhead shark,
We give thanks!

For horses and kitties,
Small bunnies and dogs,
For babies and family
And knowing we're loved,
We give thanks!

—Gail Forsyth-Vail and the children of the
North Parish of North Andover, Massachusetts

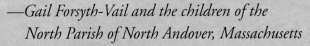

Blessings on our furry friends,
our friends who fly or crawl or swim.
Blessings on the ones we love
just because they are our friends.
Blessings on the ones we care for
And the ones who care for us,
who comfort us when we are sad,
who bark, meow, cheep or silently creep
when we come home from work and play.
Blessings on our animal friends.

—*Marguerite Sheehan*

See the kitten on the wall,
Sporting with the leaves that fall,
Withered leaves, one, two and three
Falling from the elder tree,
Through the calm and frosty air
Of the morning bright and fair.

See the kitten, how she starts,
Crouches, stretches, paws and darts;
With a tiger-leap half way
Now she meets her coming prey.
Lets it go as fast and then
Has it in her power again.

—*William Wordsworth, adapted*

A little frog sat on a log
That lay out in the sun.
He had to dive and swim to shore,
Because he couldn't run!

—*Alice Wilkins*

Brown and furry
Caterpillar in a hurry;
Take your walk
To the shady leaf or stalk.

May no toad spy you,
May the little birds pass by you;
Spin and die,
To live again a butterfly.

—*Christina Rossetti*

He knows when you're happy
He knows when you're comfortable
He knows when you're confident
And he always knows when you have carrots.

—*anonymous*

Dear God, hear and bless
Your beasts and singing birds;
And guard with tenderness
Small things that have no words.

—*anonymous*

The Spider's Prayer

No rain.
Many flies.
Gentle feet
That take no notice
Of one so small.
That's all.

—*Laura Godwin*

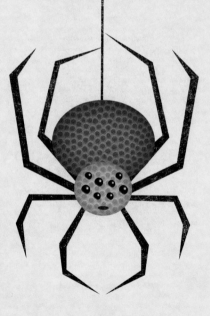

I think mice
Are rather nice.
    Their tails are long,
    Their faces small.
    They haven't any
    Chins at all.
    Their ears are pink,
    Their teeth are white,
    They run about
    The house at night.
    They nibble things they shouldn't touch
    And no one seems to like them much
But I think mice
Are nice.
—*Rose Fyleman*

When the pale moon hides and the wild wind wails,
And over the tree-tops the nighthawk sails,
The gray wolf sits on the world's far rim,
And howls: and it seems to comfort him.

The wolf is a lonely soul, you see,
No beast in the wood, nor bird in the tree,
But shuns his path; in the windy gloom
They give him plenty, and plenty of room.

So he sits with his long, lean face to the sky
Watching the ragged clouds go by.
There in the night, alone, apart,
Singing the song of his lone, wild heart.

Far away, on the world's dark rim
He howls, and it seems to comfort him.

—*Georgia Roberts Durston*

A rabbit works its ears, and tries
To watch you with its rabbit eyes,
Its saucy tail it flounces,
And when it hits the ground, it bounces!

—*Mary Carolyn Davies*

What makes the crickets "crick" all night

And never stop to rest?
They must take naps in daytime

So at night they'll "crick" their best.
I wonder if they just take turns

And try to make it rhyme,
Or do a million crickets

Keep "cricking" all the time?

—*Helen Wing*

Spirit of Life, help me remember
that all animals belong.
Bless the bats for eating mosquitoes.
Bless the crows and buzzards
for cleaning up the dead,
and bless even the snakes,
who keep the mice out of the rice.
Each of them is important.
And each does good in its own way.
Blessed be.

—*Eliza Blanchard*

How doth the little crocodile
Improve his shining tail,
And pour the waters of the Nile
On every golden scale!

How cheerfully he seems to grin,
How neatly spreads his claws,
And welcomes little fishes in,
With gently smiling jaws!

—*Lewis Carroll*

The big gray elephant slowly walks.
She doesn't make a sound.
She swings her trunk from left to right
When she puts her feet on the ground.
Swing, swing, left and right,
She doesn't make a sound.

—*anonymous*

When I grow up I want to be wise and kind.
When I grow up I want to be a friend to all—
People, animals, and Earth.
May I begin to grow up now.

—*Robin Gray*

The deer, the deer, here he went,
Here are his tracks over mother earth…
Tramping, tramping, through the deep forest.

—*Cochiti Indian poem*

If there is a god,
I think he sees the world through the eyes
of a big, brown bear
and through the eyes of a dove
and through the eyes of a gentle,
medium-size whale.

—*J. David Scheyer, adapted*

For all that dwell below the skies
Let songs of hope and faith arise
Let peace, goodwill on earth be sung
Or barked or howled by every tongue!

—*LoraKim Joyner*

Once I saw a little bird
Come hop, hop, hop,
And so I cried, Little Bird,
Will you stop, stop, stop?

I was going to the window
To say, How do you do?
But he shook his little tail,
And far away he flew.

—*anonymous*

To grass or leaf, or fruit, or wall,
The snail sticks close, nor fears to fall,
As if he grew there, house and all
Together.

—*William Cowper*

Flitting white-fire insects!
Wandering small-fire beasts!
Wave little stars about my bed!
Weave little stars into my sleep!
Come, little dancing white-fire bug,
Come, little flitting white-fire beast!
Light me with your white-flame magic,
Your little star-torch.

—*Ojibwa song*

Great Owl of Dreams,
Wings soft and furred with dark,
Soar through my sleep
To that tender place between the eyes and heart.

Bring me a dream to feed me and teach
me and guide me,
A shining star to light my soul.

—*anonymous*

Thank you for the beasts so tall
Thank you for the creatures small.
Thank you for all things that live
Thank you, God, for all you give.

—*H.W. Dobson*

Good Night, Good Night

The dark is dreaming.
Day is done.
Good night, good night
To everyone.

Good night to the birds,
And the fish in the sea,
Good night to the bears
And good night to me.

—*Dennis Lee*

Illustrations copyright © 2010 by Joyce Hesselberth

Printed in the United States

ISBN 1-55896-558-0 / 978-1-55896-558-4

13 12 11 10 / 6 5 4 3 2 1

Library of Congress Cataloging-in-Publication Data

A child's book of animal poems and blessings / collected by Eliza
Blanchard.
       p. cm.
ISBN-13: 978-1-55896-558-4 (hardcover : alk. paper)
ISBN-10: 1-55896-558-0 (hardcover : alk. paper)
1. Animals--Juvenile poetry. 2. Children's poetry. 3.
Animals—Poetry. 4. Children—Prayers and devotions. I. Blanchard,
Eliza, 1950-
  PN6110.A7C55 2010
  808.81'9362--dc22
                         2009047652

We gratefully acknowledge permission to reprint the following: prayer by Gail Forsyth-Vail and the children of the North Parish of North Andover, MA; prayer by Marguerite Sheehan; "Good Night, Good Night" from *Jelly Belly* by Dennis Lee (Macmillan of Canada, 1983; Key Porter, 2001), copyright © 1983 Dennis Lee, with permission of the author; poem by J. David Scheyer, adapted; "The Spider's Prayer" from Laura Godwin's *Barnyard Prayers*, copyright © 2000 by Laura Godwin, reprinted by permission of Disney•Hyperion, an imprint of Disney Book Group, LLC, all rights reserved; prayer by LoraKim Joyner, adapted from a doxology by Isaac Watts; prayer by H.W. Dobson, copyright © The Archbishops' Council, copyright.copyright@c-of-e.org.uk, reproduced by permission.